Wake up to the World of Science

SMALL MAMMALS

Burke Publishing Company Limited

LONDON   TORONTO   NEW YORK

First published in the English language 1988
© Burke Publishing Company Limited 1988
Translated and adapted from *Les petits mammifères* by Bornancin and Marseau
© Editions Fernand Nathan 1985

Acknowledgements
The publishers are grateful to Jennifer Dyke for preparing the text of this edition and to the following for permission to reproduce copyright illustrations:
    Lieutier - Jacana; Labat - Jacana; Labat-Ferrero - Jacana; P. Garguil; J.-P. Varin - Jacana; P. Garguil; Ermie - Jacana; Visage - Jacana; Bailleau - Jacana; Mammifrance - Jacana; Ferrero - Jacana; Arthus -Bertrand — Jacana; D et S. Simon; Bornancin — P; Ziesler - Jacana; D. Mendin; Giraudon; Tercafs -Jacana; J.-J. Soulas; A. Rainon - Jacana; Frank Lane Picture Agency Ltd.

CIP data
Bornancin, B.
    Small mammals.
    I. Mammals – For schools
    I. Title II. Marseau, S. III. Les petits mammiferes.
    English IV. Series
    599

ISBN 0 222 01481 4 Hardbound
ISBN 0 222 01482 2 Paperback

Burke Publishing Company Limited
Pegasus House, 116-120 Golden Lane, London EC1Y 0TL, England.
Burke Publishing (Canada) Limited
Registered Office: 20 Queen Street West, Suite 3000, Box 30, Toronto, Canada M5H 1V5.
Burke Publishing Company Inc.
Registered Office: 333 State Street, PO Box 1740, Bridgeport, Connecticut 06601, U.S.A.
Filmset in Souvenir by Trendsetters, Hull, England.
Printed in Spain by Graficas Reunidas

Contents

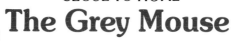

The Grey Mouse

This mouse is easily recognized by its long tail, grey fur and large ears.

It is also called the house mouse because it has lived near human settlements for thousands of years. It is a lively, agile, timid, little creature.

It comes indoors, mainly in the winter, and lives under floorboards, behind skirtings and in cupboards. If a mouse has decided to live with you, you will hear it squeaking and scampering in the evenings, and you will find little droppings beside the remains of fruits and seeds which it has nibbled. The grey mouse likes all human food, especially cereals such as wheat and maize.

Mice live in families. The female can have four to six litters a year. There are five to eight little mice per litter; they stay in the nest for about a fortnight. The nest is made of scraps of paper and cloth. The mouse has her first babies very young, when she is about ten weeks old. We would be invaded by mice if it were not for cats and birds of prey.

Question: What does each animal in this book like to eat. Classify the animals according to what they eat. Then find out what each of these animals has in common.

The Sewer Rat
or Brown Rat

The rat's nest is in a hole in a wall, amongst piles of merchandise, or in a tunnel underground. It is made of all sorts of oddments: straw, paper, cloth, etc.

The brown rat is three times the size of the mouse. Its fur is brown on its back and light grey on its belly.

This rat lives near us and eats our stores of food. It came to Europe from Asia in the thirteenth century and gradually replaced another species, the black rat, which was responsible for spreading the Plague in the Middle Ages. The brown rat is active at night. You can hear its sharp squeaks and snarls near the piles of refuse where it looks for food. It frequently leaves behind:
footmarks (see the drawing)
and small, elongated droppings.

Several families of rats live together, forming colonies with a common nest. They store a lot of food in the nest.

Like the mouse, the rat has babies all year round; it can have seven or eight young every month. The young rats are hunted by cats, dogs and birds of prey. The adults are more pugnacious. They defend themselves and will attack predators, even those larger than themselves.

For reasons of hygiene we prevent the rat population from spreading in towns, and put down poison in the places where rats live.

The Common Dormouse

The common dormouse is easily recognized by its reddish-brown colour, plump body, round ears and short legs. Its neck and chest are white and the tip of the tail may also be white.

Dormice live in trees and shrubs, in gardens, woods and even mountain forests. They come out at night to look for food, and will eat seeds, nuts, berries and insects. The common dormouse is also sometimes known as the hazel dormouse because of its liking for hazelnuts and the fact that it often lives in hazel copses. It is known as an excellent climber although it makes its nest near to (or below) the ground.

At the end of the summer it gathers fruits and seeds together in its nest of dry grasses in the trunk of a tree or a hole in the ground.

As soon as the weather begins to get colder, the dormice roll up into a ball, one beside the other, and go to sleep. Their body temperature drops along with the temperature outside: this is called hibernation.

At the end of the winter, the dormice will have lost a lot of weight. As the weather gets warmer they become active again and the female has a litter of three or four young during the summer. The babies are born naked and blind but within eighteen days they open their eyes.

The Pipistrelle Bat

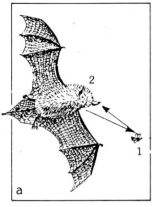

The bat makes ultrasonic squeaks which spread through the air and bounce back from any solid object, such as an insect on the wing (1) or a wall. By interpreting the time taken for the echo to return (2) the bat locates its prey (the insect) or is warned of a danger (the wall).

The pipistrelle is the smallest and most widespread of the European bats.

It comes out on summer evenings at dusk, when you can see its jerky, zigzag flight. How is it able to avoid obstacles and catch insects in the dark? As it flies it makes sharp squeaks which we can hear and other, sharper squeaks which we cannot hear. They are ultrasounds (a).

During the summer the pipistrelle lives in trees and cracks in walls. In winter it looks for a more sheltered spot, such as a barn or a cave where it can hibernate. The bats spend the winter hanging upside-down in their hiding-place.

At the beginning of summer, the females come together and give birth to between one and three young ones each. The young bats are all reared together.

There are many superstitions about bats. They do no harm, however, and are astonishing little creatures with their soft fur and large wings made from a thin, yet tough and supple membrane.

Although they have wings, bats are mammals, because the females suckle their young.

Question: What is a bat's wing made of? Describe its shape.

The Harvest Mouse

The fur of this mouse is reddish brown on top and white beneath.

The harvest mouse is the smallest European rodent. It lives in meadows, cornfields, ditches and hedges. It feeds, especially at night, on fruits, seeds, buds and insects.

It is very agile and climbs up the grasses with the help of its tail, which curls around the stems amongst which it hides during the day (see the photo). The harvest mouse is not very easily seen, but can be heard squeaking. You may also find its nest: a ball of dried grass, about ten centimetres (four inches) in diameter hanging in the long grass. The nest is made by the female to give birth to between three and seven young. She has two or three litters during the summer.

During the winter the whole family takes up residence in a more comfortable nest underground, or in a bale of hay or a barn. A few stores are gathered together at the beginning of the winter, but the harvest mouse remains active all year round.

It is prey to a number of creatures: small carnivores or birds of prey such as buzzards and falcons. Its greatest enemy is the farmer, who destroys its nests with combine harvesters, and tears up the hedges where it may also have its nest. The harvest mouse population is, therefore, growing smaller.

The Field Mouse

This is the commonest small mammal in Europe, easily recognized by its large ears, wide eyes and long tail which helps it to climb. Its belly is silver grey with a small yellow patch on the chest.

The field mouse lives in hedges and brushwood, and sometimes in gardens, where it hollows out little tunnels to serve as a nest and a larder for provisions. Look for the entrances to these tunnels which are three or four centimetres (just over one inch) in diameter; you will recognize them by the big pile of loose soil in front of them.

The field mouse is nocturnal and comes out at nightfall to look for nuts and seeds, insects and dead animals, particularly hedgehogs. Their bounding tracks look like small cloven hoof marks.

The field mouse has many enemies, notably cats and birds of prey. It is active all year round, the female giving birth several times a year to between four and seven young.

The Field Vole

This rodent has small ears and a short tail. Its fur is short, dark brown above, grey/white below (a).

Voles live in a large groups in fields, meadows and damp pastures. They are especially active at dawn and dusk, but leave their holes several times during the day (b).

The vole breeds all year round. Young voles can have babies themselves as early as six weeks old.

In some areas, voles are very numerous and would be a plague on cereal crops if they did not have so many enemies: small carnivores, foxes, birds of prey. (An owl will eat on average 1,500 voles a year.) Voles are also killed off by the cold and wet in winter: their holes and runways turn to ice.

a

b

The Wild Rabbit

The rabbit lives in dry, sandy places, where it digs complex burrows 40 to 50 centimetres (15 to 20 inches) deep. (The rabbit in the photo is about to leave its burrow).

Rabbits are sociable creatures which live as a family (one male and several females). Rabbit families join together to form larger groups with communicating burrows. They occupy a large territory, as much as 500 metres (over 1,600 feet) around the burrow, and mark the boundary with piles of droppings in the form of small pellets. This wide area in which a colony of rabbits lives is called a warren. The rabbits come out towards the end of the afternoon and nibble methodically at the grass around them. They are shy creatures and sound the alarm by thumping on the ground with their hind-legs. You can hear this noise, like a drum roll, when you approach a warren.

The female rabbits have five or six litters of five or six young each year. They give birth in a separate burrow, just under the surface, called a "stab" or a "stop" (see the pictures). The baby rabbits are born naked and blind. They stay in the nest (made of dry grass and fur stripped from the female's own belly) for four weeks.

Rabbits are eaten by many carnivorous animals and by human beings. In the early 1950s a contagious disease, known as myxomatosis, was introduced into Europe to reduce the rabbit population, because rabbits were damaging crops. The disease has proved very difficult to control, and even domesticated rabbits have been infected. The rabbit has been domesticated for over a thousand years.

The Hare

The hare is larger than the wild rabbit. It is easily identified by its long, black-pointed ears, and the top side of its tail which is also black.

The hare is a solitary creature which is most active at night. It fashions a hollow, or "form", at ground level which retains the shape of its body. Here the hare lies motionless, the colour of its fur well camouflaged against the grass.

The site of the form varies with the seasons. During the summer the hare is found in the fields and meadows, eating grass and other crops. In the winter it moves into the woods and gnaws the bark off the trees. You may see its footprints in the snow. It hops along, twisting and turning to confuse its predators — foxes, wild cats, the larger birds of prey and human beings.

Hares only come together during the breeding season at the end of winter. Their behaviour is very aggressive at this time, and the pre-mating antics of the males include bounding and chasing, kicking and boxing. The female hare, called a doe, gives birth to between two and four leverets directly onto the ground. They are born with a covering of fur and they leave the mother after three weeks. There are three or four litters each year.

Hares are very numerous and cause a lot of damage to farmland. They are actively hunted. The species survives thanks to its great fertility, and also its regular re-introduction into the countryside by hunting societies. (There are places in Central Europe where hares are specially bred for this purpose.)

11

 # The Hedgehog

The hedgehog is known for the spines on its back and its pointed nose. When it senses danger, it gathers its legs up beneath its belly and rolls itself into a ball. All that can be seen is its spines sticking out like a pincushion. It doesn't move.

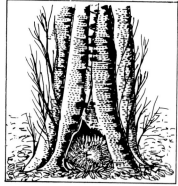

The hedgehog stays in its nest during the day. The nest is made of a pile of dry leaves and grasses, lined with moss. It is placed on the ground in the shelter of a bush, an old wall or a pile of wood. Near the nest you can see small, black, shiny droppings, full of insect remains.

The hedgehog emerges at sunset to look for food, scampering along on its short legs. It has a varied diet of insects, worms, small rodents, small birds and, rarely, snakes. It will also eat eggs, fruit and dead animals. It makes a noise as it moves along, grunting and squeaking. You can often hear it if you walk alongside a hedge at nightfall. But don't try to catch a hedgehog. It needs a much bigger territory than a mere garden.

During its nightly expeditions, the hedgehog is in danger of being run over by traffic as it crosses the road. It may also be captured by a fox, badger or bird of prey.

It takes to its nest between the months of October and March, after eating sufficient to accumulate a layer of fat (it may weigh more than a kilo – over two pounds – at this time). It wakes up from time to time. It hibernates like the bat.

The female hedgehog gives birth to one or two litters of between three and seven baby hedgehogs during the summer (a); the babies have soft spines (b) and can roll themselves into a ball at eleven days old.

b

The Mole

The mole announces its presence with mounds of soil, or molehills, in fields or gardens.

The mole is an animal with short black fur. It lives underground, where it digs very extensive tunnels. Its nest is a large cavity deep in the centre of the tunnel system (as much as 60 centimetres – over 23 inches – down) lined with dry grass and sometimes known as a "fortress" (a).

The tunnels are used for hunting. The mole finds its food as it digs its way through the soil. It works very quickly, digging a tunnel 12 to 15 metres (40 to 50 feet) long in an hour if the ground is soft. Molehills are formed by the earth thrown out onto the surface when the tunnels are made.

The mole feeds on any creatures it comes across, especially earthworms, which account for ninety-five per cent of its food. Moles are blind and find their food by a well-developed sense of smell, hearing and touch. They detect the presence of earthworms by the vibrations the worms make as they move through the soil.

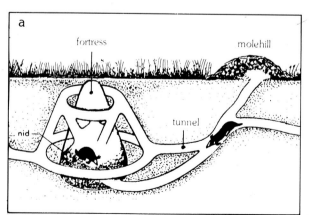

The females have only one litter per year, in spring, consisting of between two and six young. They grow very rapidly and are adult-sized in two months. Very exceptionally, in dry weather, the mole will come above ground to look for food, because the worms have buried themselves too deeply in the soil.

The mole is hunted because its molehills make the fields difficult to work, and because the tunnels cut through the roots of growing crops. However, the mole does a good job by loosening the soil deep down and eating pests such as snails, slugs and grubs.

Question: Can you explain why we say the mole is a burrowing animal, well-adapted to life underground?

The Shrew

The shrew is a lively little animal. Its long, pointed snout distinguishes it from similar-sized mammals such as field mice and voles.

The shrew makes its home amongst dry leaves, often in the holes of other small mammals.

Like the mole, it hunts for food several times a day. It eats insects, spiders and worms which live above ground like itself. It will also eat dead creatures. It consumes its own weight in food in a day.

Its enemies are birds of prey, such as the barn owl. But carnivorous animals will not eat it because of its smell.

The shrew has a short life-span. But this is made up for by the large number of young ones born between April and September: three litters of between five and six young ones each.

The Stone Marten

- Chestnut fur and white bib (a).
- Lives in rocky areas, and shelters in a hole. It is also found close to human habitation, in barns, gardens and bales of hay or straw.
- It is very numerous; living in closer and closer proximity to man.
- Hunts at night for small rodents; also visits hen-houses!

The Pine Marten

- Chestnut fur with a yellow patch on the throat (b).
- Lives in forests; a very acrobatic climber which nests in the trunks of trees. Likes to sun itself on a branch.
- It is active both by day and by night, and hunts squirrels and dormice. Very fond of small birds, eggs and fruit.
- Endangered species.

The Weasel

- In summer, brown back and white belly (c). White fur in winter.
- Active during the day and evening, in fields and woods, but also close to human habitation. It can often be seen racing across a road or footpath.
- Because of its small size, it can enter the holes of small rodents, which it kills with a bite on the back of the neck.
- The stoat looks very similar, but is larger.

The Polecat

- Also called "foul-marten" because of the unpleasant smell it gives off when in danger (d).
- Lives in wooded regions, in coppices, close to water where food debris and droppings can be seen.
- It is very aggressive, hunting at night for rodents such as rabbits and rats. Also eats eggs.
- The ferret, which has been domesticated, looks very like the polecat, but its colour varies a great deal.

b   a

c   d

The Squirrel

a

The squirrel is recognized by its big bushy tail, small round head and ears with a very long tuft of hair on the tips in winter, red back and white belly (a).

The squirrel lives in the trees and is active during the day. It runs up and down the trunks of the trees clinging on to the bark with its strong, curved claws. It jumps from one tree to another, with its long tail acting as a rudder (b). It takes small hops on the ground. Its footprints can be seen in the snow in winter.

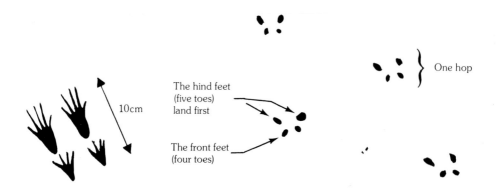

10cm

The hind feet (five toes) land first

The front feet (four toes)

One hop

Squirrel footprints in the snow

The squirrel makes a large nest in the fork of a branch near the trunk. It sleeps there at night. In the winter it makes or finds another, stronger nest in which it can remain for several days at a time. It does not hibernate, but dozes with its tail wrapped around.

In the forest, the squirrel finds plenty of food of all kinds: young shoots in the spring, mushrooms and nuts in the autumn, fir cones, pine cones, snails, insects, birds' eggs. It sits up on its hind-legs, holds its food in its front paws and crunches it with its strong front teeth.

You will see a lot of things which it has dropped, such as this hazelnut shell.

In the month of August, when there is plenty of food about, the squirrel begins to gather a store of food and buries it in the ground. It doesn't always find it again in the winter! And the seeds buried in the soil in this way will germinate in the spring. So, thanks to its forgetfulness, the squirrel helps to plant new trees. This contribution to the life of the forest makes up a little for the damage the squirrel causes in spring by eating buds and young shoots.

Depending upon the climate and where it lives, the squirrel has one or two litters a year, of three or four young. Their mother rears them in a nest and they leave the nest at the age of one and a half months.

The enemies of the squirrel are the martens, which also live in the trees, and birds of prey.

The Fox

a

The red fox has a pointed face, large ears and bushy tail (a).

Stories and fables would have us believe that the fox is a creature capable of escaping every trap that can be set. The fox isn't really any more cunning than other animals, but it knows its own territory very well, it moves about quickly and seems to have a good memory. If it senses danger, it prefers to run away rather than hide.

Like many other carnivores the fox marks its territory; to do this it uses a smelly secretion produced by glands on its hind-legs and beneath its tail. You can follow its trail by the strong scent of its urine and droppings. The droppings have a long

spiral shape. The fox's food varies according to the time of year; in the summer it will eat insects and small birds; in the autumn it will gorge itself on fruits. Throughout the year it eats a great many small rodents (including rabbits and voles) which do a lot of damage to crops. It also eats sick animals and rotting flesh or carrion. The natural predators of the fox, the wolf and the lynx have all but disappeared from Europe, although in Africa large carnivores still hunt the fox.

The fox is often accused of robbing poultry-houses and game-reserves, also of spreading rabies. Therefore it is hunted all year round. But, in spite of this, it comes closer and closer to human habitation.

The fox may dig an earth (b) but is more likely to occupy one made by another creature, such as a badger or rabbit, which it enlarges. The entrance to the earth is littered with heaps of soil, food debris and trampled grass and marked by a strong smell of urine.

You can identify the fox's footprints in the snow.

The fox lives alone and hunts mainly at night. It finds a mate during the winter. It is then that foxes can be heard yelping in the woods. Three or four young foxes are born in the spring and are trained by the female for six months before they become adult.

The fox loses its thick winter fur in the summer, and looks a bit like a mangy dog. We say that it moults.

Foxes may be found up to 3,000 metres (nearly 10,000 feet) up in the mountains. They don't deserve the bad reputation they have of being destructive.

Question: What does the fox eat? Draw up a food chain containing the fox. Do you know why the fox is so successful in this country?

Foxes on the alert at the entrance to their earth

b

 # The Badger

The badger looks and walks a little like a bear, but is much smaller and lives in the open countryside. It is easily recognized by its long white head with two broad black stripes over the eyes and ears. Its stiff grey hair has been used to make shaving-brushes and paint-brushes.

The badger moves about rather heavily on its short legs (a) and leaves large footprints.

The badger seeks its food (and visits other badgers) at night. Badgers live as a family in large underground setts, with many entrances and airholes. They take refuge in the sett at the least sign of danger. The entrance to the sett is marked by a sort of slide or chute created by the badger from earth and stones thrown out of the sett. In the entrance there is straw and moss which has dropped off the pile of "bedding" carried down to the chamber where the badgers live. Quite close to the sett can be found the "latrines" which the badgers dig to dispose of their urine and faeces.

The badger scratches the ground and turns over stones to look for worms, insects, small rodents or carrion.

It eats a lot of grass, fruits and roots and is very fond of wasps nests.

It puts on a good layer of fat in the autumn.

These fat reserves enable it to remain in its sett for several weeks during the winter without coming out to feed.

The female badger (or sow) has just one litter a year, towards the end of the winter, consisting of between one and four young (cubs). The cubs are very playful and stay with their parents until the autumn (b). They are very fond of water (c).

In our part of the world, the badgers' natural predators (the wolf and the lynx) are extinct, but badgers are hunted by large carnivores in Asia.

The badger's greatest enemy is the farmer and the gamekeeper, who accuse it of destroying game, damaging crops and carrying rabies. That is why the badger population is shrinking rapidly in certain areas.

Questions: How does the behaviour of the badger compare with that of the fox? Which mammals dig burrows, and what are their burrows used for?

b

c

The Wild Cat

a

The wild cat resembles the domesticated tabby, but is more heavily built with well-defined black stripes. It has a short, bushy tail with a round black tip (a). The head is large with small ears which it flattens when danger threatens (b, see its fangs too).

The wild cat has been accused of eating hares, rabbits, small squirrels, and even of attacking human beings. Recent studies, however, have shown that it stalks and eats mainly small rodents.

It lives alone or with a mate in hollow trees or holes in the rocks. It can climb trees to rob nests, to rest or to hide, but climbs down rather clumsily. It is a very cautious animal and not easy to see.

The wild cat has three or four kittens a year at the end of spring, and although once common has become very rare.

Question: How does the wild cat hunt its prey? Find out how the other carnivores in this book hunt their prey.

The Genet

a

The genet is a strange animal, looking like a cross between a cat and a stone marten. The head tapers to a pointed muzzle and the ears are large. The long, furry tail is ringed with dark and light bands. Its grey, dappled fur is much sought after (a).

Genets may live alone, or as a family, in hollow trees or holes in the rocks, like the wild cat. They hunt at night for small rodents, birds, snakes, lizards and insects.

The female has two litters a year of between one and three young, in the spring and again at the end of the summer.

The genet was very widespread during the Middle Ages, living close to human settlements – it was domesticated before the cat to hunt the mice in houses. Its name is mentioned in old stories, and it is depicted with other domestic animals on a famous fifteenth-century tapestry called *The Lady and the Unicorn* (b).

Although considered for a long time as a harmful animal, the genet is today a protected species. Distribution is uneven, with the genet being common in some areas and absent in others.

b

The Coypu, an invader

a

This large rodent is a native of South America, and was introduced into Europe in the nineteenth century to be bred for its fur, known as nutria. But some coypus were released from the farms (and some escaped) and returned to the wild. It is the descendants of these escapees which now populate a large number of watercourses and marshy areas.

Coypus live near rivers, dykes and canals (a) and dig long burrows in the banks. At the point where they enter the water, the earth is trodden down and the grass cut. The prints of their large paws and claws can be seen. Food debris can also be seen: stalks, broken roots, sweet-corn cores; also their cylindrical, chestnut-brown droppings, the surface of which is finely ridged.

The coypu is particularly active at dusk. It is not at all shy and will wash and groom itself for quite a while beside its burrow. It waddles with a humped back through fields and meadows in search of plants to eat. It swims well with its head above the water (b).

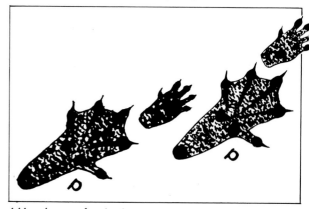

The hind-feet are webbed like those of a duck.

It eats a great deal of vegetable matter which it bites off with its powerful, orange-red front teeth. It can eat up to thirty per cent of its weight in food a day.

The female coypu usually has two litters of five or six babies a year, at the end of the winter and during the autumn. The babies are well-developed at birth and stay with the mother for three months.

Natural predators are rare in this part of the world because the coypu is an introduced species; occasionally a fox or an otter will attack a coypu. The cold in winter and drought in summer are a significant cause of death.

In certain areas, people have to limit the coypu population because of the damage to crops and river banks.

And yet their fur is sought after, and they do a good job clearing watercourses choked by vegetation during the summer.

Question: If a child weighs 30 kilos (over 66 pounds) and eats like a coypu, that is to say thirty per cent of its weight in food a day, how much food does it swallow in one day?

As it swims, the coypu breathes in air through its nostrils. Note its big orange-red front teeth.

b

The Otter, a protected species

The otter lives near rivers, lakes and marshes (a). It can be recognized by its pretty, rounded head, small ears and long whiskers. Its thick waterproof fur is brown on top and pale beneath.

It swims well (c) thanks to its long, supple body, webbed feet and rudder-like tail. It can remain under water for six to seven minutes and dive to a depth of 10 metres (over 32 feet).

The otter has its territory along a stretch of the river bank. It lives beneath a rock, in a tree stump or in an earth abandoned by some other creature. It moves overland by humping its back. It can also stand upright (b).

Often nocturnal, the otter uses many ingenious hunting techniques, chasing its prey, or stalking and lying in wait. Its long whiskers help it to detect prey. It captures fish of all sorts, crayfish, waterbirds and small rodents (including rabbits and voles).

The otter sometimes leaves food remains on stones sticking out of the water or in the grass along the banks. Its droppings are always found in one place, in a very obvious position, on a stone or in the grass.

The female otter has one litter a year of from two to four babies. She teaches them how to fish and live in the water. She leaves them when their schooling is finished, after six or seven months. This long schooling of otter babies by their mother is something quite rare.

Another peculiarity of the otter is its love of play. It will often make slides down the banks or in the snow and use them for sliding games.

The otter is very resistant to cold and is able to fish in frozen lakes.

b

The otter is an endangered species. It has been hunted and trapped for its fur and because it competes with fishermen for fish. It has also been a victim of water pollution and the destruction of its natural habitat. It survives in a few regions, where it is protected because it is considered to play an important role by eating sick creatures or those existing in too great a number.

Question: Why would you say that the otter is well adapted to living in the water?

Otter playing in the water

c

Answers to Questions

page 4 **Classifying mammals according to their food**

They eat mainly plants	They eat mainly animals	
	Insects, larvae, worms, snails . . .	small mammals, birds, fish . . .
mouse, brown rat, dormouse, harvest mouse, field mouse, vole, rabbit, hare, squirrel, coypu.	bat, hedgehog, mole, shrew	stone marten, pine marten, stoat, weasel, polecat, ferret, genet, wild cat, fox, badger, otter.
They gnaw stems and seeds with their long front teeth. They are rodents (see the coypu – page 26).	They tear their prey to pieces with their many little pointed teeth. They are insectivores.	They bite the flesh off with their fangs, and grind it in their big molars. They are carnivores (see the wild cat – page 24).

All these animals have fur, and the females suckle their young.
They are mammals.

page 7 A bat's wing

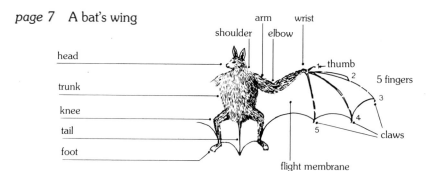

The bat's wing is formed by the upper arm, forearm and hand. The wing membrane extends between the fingers, the limbs and the trunk.

page 15 The life of the mole

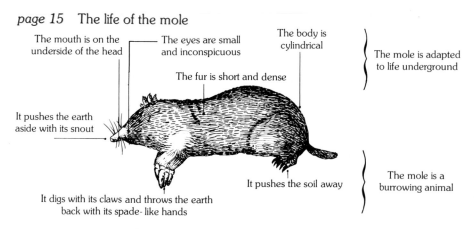

The mouth is on the underside of the head

The eyes are small and inconspicuous

The body is cylindrical

The fur is short and dense

The mole is adapted to life underground

It pushes the earth aside with its snout

It digs with its claws and throws the earth back with its spade-like hands

It pushes the soil away

The mole is a burrowing animal

page 21 A food chain which includes the fox

grass ——————▶ the rabbit ——————▶ the fox ——————▶ the wolf
　　　(is eaten by)　　　　　(is eaten by)　　　　　(is eaten by)

Foxes are widespread in this part of the world because their natural enemies (the wolf and the lynx) are extinct.

page 23 The badger and the fox

	appearance, manner	lives	when disturbed
fox	slender, alert, quick	alone	runs away
badger	squat, clumsy, hesitant	in a family group	takes refuge in its sett

page 23 Small mammals and their holes

Holes may be used for shelter, as a larder, or as a nest for the young.				
For these animals	The hole is used for	shelter	larder	nest
brown rat, field mouse		X	X	X
harvest mouse (in winter)		X		
field vole, rabbit, mole, fox, badger, coypu, stone-marten		X		

page 24 How carnivores hunt

Weasel, polecat	They hunt rodents in their tunnels or on the ground
badger	It digs in the soil
fox	It runs and jumps on its prey
cat	It stalks its prey along the ground
stone-marten	It hunts its prey amongst rocks and around buildings
genet, pine-marten	They hunt their prey in trees and bushes
otter	It chases or stalks its prey, in the water

page 27 The coypu

If a child weighing 30 kilos (over 66 pounds) ate like the coypu, it would consume thirty per cent of its weight in one day, that is 9 kilos (nearly 20 pounds) of food!

page 29 The otter

It has a long, supple body, covered with waterproof fur.

Its long tail acts as a rudder

Its webbed feet help it to swim

Authors' Note

It's easy to spot a mouse, a squirrel or a hedgehog. But many small mammals are quite difficult to see: they are very shy and may only come out of their holes at night. On the other hand, you can see signs of them very easily: footprints in the mud or snow, food debris, trampled vegetation, hairs caught on twigs and branches, droppings, etc. They are all clues to the identity of the creature which has passed that way. Then, with the help of your own observations and the information in this book, you will discover that many of these creatures have very large families, and consequently we must protect their predators — the animals which feed on them: Others are becoming very rare and must themselves be protected.

Whatever they are, all small mammals play an important role in the balance of nature and, to understand this role, it is useful to find out more about them.